MARGARET FULTON
COOKING FOR TWO

MARGARET FULTON'S BOOK OF COOKING FOR TWO

OCTOPUS

CONTENTS

Breakfasts	6
Fish	14
Meat & poultry	24
Egg & cheese dishes	46
Vegetables & salads	56
Desserts	74
Index	94

This edition published 1989
by Octopus Illustrated Publishing
Michelin House, 81 Fulham Road
London SW3 6RB
part of Reed International Books

Reprinted 1991, 1992

Copyright © Reed International Books Limited 1980

ISBN 0 7064 5012 4

Produced by Mandarin Offset
Printed and bound in Hong Kong

INTRODUCTION

Here is a book written for that ever-growing band of people who are cooking for two. It is a book to reassure you that meals can always be varied, appetising and adventurous as well as nutritious whether you are cooking for one, two or a big family.

There are suggestions for breakfasts, snacks, light suppers; for wintry days there are lovely casseroles and hotpots, lots of unusual ways of cooking chicken, and some really super salads. If you like desserts there are many you can make for two. You can enjoy Plum Tart, Banana Orange Caramel Creams or lovely Date and Lemon Pudding and learn to make an impressive souffle omelet.

Most of the recipes are quick and easy to make, others require a little forward planning. Whatever the occasion this practical cookbook will provide a source of inspiration when cooking for two.

Margaret Fulton

NOTE
Standard spoon and cup measurements are used in all recipes
1 tablespoon = one 20 ml spoon
1 teaspoon = one 5 ml spoon
All spoon measures are level
1 cup = 250 ml.

Fresh herbs are used unless otherwise stated. If unobtainable substitute a bouquet garni of the equivalent dried herbs, or use dried herbs instead but halve the quantities stated.

Use freshly ground black pepper where pepper is specified.

Ovens should be preheated to the specified temperature.

For all recipes, quantities are given in both metric and imperial measures. Follow either set but not a mixture of both, because they are not interchangeable.

All recipes serve 2 unless otherwise stated.

BREAKFASTS

Tangy Grapefruit

1 grapefruit, halved
2-3 tablespoons raisins
4 tablespoons natural low-fat yogurt
1-2 tablespoons brown sugar (optional)

Cut the segments from each grapefruit half, discarding the pith and reserving the shells. Place the segments in a bowl and stir in the raisins and yogurt.

Pile the mixture into the grapefruit shells and sprinkle with sugar, if preferred. Chill in the refrigerator overnight.

Bran Yogurt

1 banana, sliced
⅔ cup mandarin yogurt
1-2 tablespoons chopped hazelnuts
2 tablespoons bran

Divide the banana between two bowls. Top with the yogurt and sprinkle with the hazelnuts and bran.

Muesli

4 tablespoons rolled oats
2 tablespoons bran
2 tablespoons sultanas
1 tablespoon brown sugar
1 tablespoon mixed nuts, toasted
¾-1¼ cups milk to serve

Place the rolled oats, bran, sultanas, sugar and nuts in a bowl. Mix well and divide between 2 serving dishes. Add the milk just before serving.

Cereal Medley

2 crushed Weet Bix
1 cup cornflakes
3 tablespoons
  All-Bran
½ dessert apple,
  peeled, cored and
  grated
2 teaspoons brown
  sugar
2 tablespoons fruit
  yogurt
milk to serve

Place all the ingredients except the yogurt and milk in a bowl. Mix well and divide between 2 serving dishes. Spoon the yogurt over and serve with milk.

Milk and Orange Nog

1¼ cups chilled milk
1 egg
2 tablespoons mandarin yogurt
grated rind and juice of 1 orange
1 teaspoon honey
grated nutmeg

Whisk together the milk and egg, then add the yogurt, orange rind, juice and honey. Continue whisking until well blended.

Pour into tumblers and sprinkle with nutmeg to taste.

Kipper Toast

1 × 185 g (6 oz) packet kipper fillets with butter
grated rind and juice of 1 lemon
1 tablespoon chopped parsley
pepper
2 slices wholemeal bread, toasted
parsley sprigs to garnish

Cook the kipper fillets according to the packet instructions.

Place the fish in a bowl and mash with a fork. Add the lemon rind, juice, parsley and pepper to taste. Mix well, then divide the mixture between the toast slices.

Place under a preheated medium grill for 4 to 5 minutes. Garnish with parsley sprigs and serve immediately.

Beany Breakfast

1 × 225 g can baked beans
1 hard-boiled egg, chopped
60 g (2 oz) cooked ham, chopped
1 teaspoon Worcestershire sauce
½ teaspoon made mustard
2 teaspoons tomato ketchup or sauce
salt and pepper
2 slices bread, toasted
15 g (½ oz) butter

Place the beans in a saucepan with the egg, ham, Worcestershire sauce, mustard and tomato ketchup. Heat gently and add salt and pepper to taste.

Spread the toast with the butter and pile the bean mixture on top. Serve immediately.

Onion and Tomato Scramble

3 eggs
2 tablespoons cream
salt and pepper
30 g (1 oz) butter
½ small onion, finely chopped
1 tomato, skinned and chopped
2 slices bread, toasted

Beat the eggs with the cream and salt and pepper to taste.

Melt half the butter in a small saucepan, add the onion and fry until soft. Pour in the egg mixture and stir slowly over a gentle heat until scrambled. Stir in the tomato and remove from the heat.

Spread the toast with the remaining butter and pile the scrambled egg mixture on top. Serve immediately.

Lancashire Buns

15 g (½ oz) butter
125 g (4 oz) Lancashire cheese, grated
½ teaspoon French mustard
1 teaspoon milk
salt and pepper
2 soft rolls
1 tomato, skinned and sliced
parsley sprigs to garnish

Melt the butter in a saucepan and add the cheese. Cook over a low heat, stirring, until the cheese has melted. Stir in the mustard, milk and salt and pepper to taste.

Slice the rolls in half and toast the cut side. Spread with the cheese mixture and top with the tomato slices. Place under a preheated medium grill for 2 to 3 minutes. Garnish with parsley. Serve immediately.

Sausage Parcels

4 pork sausages
English mustard
60 g (2 oz) Cheddar cheese
2 streaky bacon rashers, derinded and halved

Cook the sausages under a preheated medium grill for 10 to 15 minutes, turning to brown evenly. Spread with mustard to taste.

Cut the cheese into 4 strips and press onto the sausages. Wrap a piece of bacon around each sausage.

Return to the grill and cook for a further 10 minutes, turning once.

Serve with grilled tomatoes or baked beans.

FISH

Mullet with Gooseberries

2 mullet, filleted
1 tablespoon fine oatmeal
salt and pepper
knob of butter
SAUCE:
125 g (4 oz) frozen gooseberries
1 tablespoon water
1 teaspoon sugar
pinch of grated nutmeg

Rinse and dry the mullet fillets. Season the oatmeal with salt and pepper to taste and sprinkle over the mackerel. Dot with butter and cook under a preheated medium grill for 15 to 20 minutes.

To make the sauce: Put all the ingredients in a saucepan. Cover and simmer for 10 to 15 minutes until the fruit is soft.

Cool slightly, then rub through a sieve or work in an electric blender until smooth and strain to remove pips.

Place the mullet on a warmed serving dish. Pour over the sauce. Serve immediately.

Fish with Sour Cream and Mushrooms

300 g (10 oz) fish fillets
salt and pepper
knob of butter
4 tablespoons water
SAUCE:
15 g (½ oz) butter
60 g (2 oz) button mushrooms, sliced
½ cup sour cream
¼ teaspoon paprika
TO GARNISH:
chopped parsley

Place the fish in a shallow 2 cup ovenproof dish. Sprinkle with salt and pepper, dot with the butter and add the water. Cover with foil and cook in a preheated moderate oven, 160°C (325°F), for 15 minutes.

Meanwhile, make the sauce: Melt the butter in a saucepan, add the mushrooms and fry for 1 minute. Stir in the sour cream, paprika and salt and pepper to taste. Heat through gently.

Drain the fish and transfer to a warmed serving dish. Pour over the sauce and garnish with chopped parsley. Serve immediately.

Fish with Lemon and Watercress Sauce

2 fish steaks
1 small onion, sliced
1 bay leaf
4 black peppercorns
grated rind of ½ lemon
3 tablespoons dry cider
salt and pepper
SAUCE:
2 teaspoons cornflour
1 teaspoon lemon juice
1 egg yolk
4 tablespoons milk
½ bunch watercress, stalks removed
TO GARNISH:
watercress sprigs

Place the fish in a shallow 2 cup ovenproof dish. Add the onion, bay leaf, peppercorns, lemon rind, cider and salt to taste. Cover with foil and cook in a preheated moderate oven, 160°C (325°F), for 20 minutes.

Transfer the fish to a warmed serving dish, discarding any skin and bones; keep hot. Strain the fish liquor and add water if necessary to make up to 5 tablespoons; cool. Blend the cornflour with the fish liquor and lemon juice. Heat, stirring, until thickened. Beat the egg yolk and milk together, then add to the sauce.

Finely chop the watercress leaves. Add to the sauce with salt and pepper to taste. Heat gently but do not boil.

Pour the sauce over the fish. Serve immediately, garnished with watercress.

Bream with Banana and Nuts

300 g (10 oz) bream fillet
15 g (½ oz) butter
1 banana, sliced
25 g (1 oz) peanuts
¼ cup ground Cheddar cheese
SAUCE:
15 g (½ oz) butter
2 tablespoons plain flour
¾ cup milk
2 tablespoons natural low-fat yogurt
salt and pepper
TO GARNISH:
parsley sprigs

Place the fish in a greased shallow ovenproof dish. Dot with the butter and cook in a preheated moderate oven, 180°C (350°F), for 10 minutes. Remove from the oven and arrange the banana and nuts over the fish.

To make the sauce: Melt the butter in a saucepan and stir in the flour. Cook for 1 minute, then gradually blend in the milk. Heat, stirring until the sauce thickens. Stir in the yogurt, with salt and pepper to taste.

Pour the sauce over the fish, sprinkle with the cheese and return to the oven for 15 minutes.

Garnish with parsley. Serve immediately.

Herb Fish Cakes

300 g (10 oz) potatoes, chopped
1 small onion, sliced
salt and pepper
1 tablespoon milk
15 g (½ oz) butter
250 g (8 oz) white fish fillet, skinned and chopped
2 teaspoons chopped parsley
½ teaspoon dried mixed herbs
1 egg, separated
dry breadcrumbs for coating
oil for shallow frying
parsley sprigs to garnish

Cook the potatoes and onion in boiling salted water until soft. Drain and mash, then beat in the milk.

Melt the butter in a saucepan, add the fish and fry for 10 to 15 minutes or until tender. Flake the fish and add to the potato. Stir in the herbs, egg yolk and salt and pepper to taste. Mix well, then leave to cool.

On a floured surface, divide the mixture into 4 and shape each piece into a flat cake. Lightly beat the egg white. Dip the fish cakes into the egg white, then coat with breadcrumbs.

Heat the oil in a frying pan and fry the fish cakes until crisp and golden. Transfer to a warmed serving dish and garnish with parsley. Serve immediately.

Kipper Vol-au-Vent

½ × 250 g packet frozen puff pastry, thawed
90 g (3 oz) kipper fillets
15 g (½ oz) butter
2 tablespoons plain flour
¾ cup milk
¼ cup grated Cheddar cheese
2 teaspoons chopped parsley
salt and pepper

Roll out the pastry to a 15 cm (6 inch) circle. Using an 8.5 cm (3½ inch) cutter, mark a circle in the centre, cutting halfway through the pastry.

Place on a baking tray and cook in a preheated hot oven, 220°C (425°F), for 20 minutes.

Cook the kipper fillets under a preheated medium grill for 2 to 3 minutes on each side, then flake.

Melt the butter in a saucepan and stir in the flour. Cook for 1 minute, then gradually blend in the milk. Heat, stirring, until the sauce thickens. Stir in the fish, cheese, parsley and salt and pepper to taste. Heat gently, stirring, until the cheese has melted.

When cooked, ease out the vol-au-vent lid and discard any soft pastry in the centre. Fill the case with the kipper mixture and replace the lid. Serve hot.

Crispy Tangy Fish

15 g (½ oz) butter
2 tablespoons plain flour
¾ cup milk
1 tablespoon mayonnaise (see page 73)
½ teaspoon lemon juice
salt and pepper
250 g (8 oz) white fish fillet
¼ cup breadcrumbs
25 g (1 oz) streaky bacon, derinded and chopped
¼ cup grated Cheddar cheese
TO GARNISH:
tomato slices

Melt the butter in a saucepan, stir in the flour and cook for 1 minute. Gradually blend in the milk and heat, stirring, until the sauce thickens. Stir in the mayonnaise, lemon juice and salt and pepper to taste.

Divide the fish into 2 pieces, place in a shallow ovenproof dish and pour over the sauce. Combine the breadcrumbs, bacon and cheese and sprinkle over the sauce.

Cook in a preheated moderately hot oven, 190°C (375°F), for 20 minutes, then place under a preheated medium grill for 2 to 3 minutes to brown the topping.

Garnish with tomato slices. Serve immediately.

Pilchard and Egg Supper

1 × 210 g can pilchards in tomatoes
1 hard-boiled egg
1 celery stick, chopped
½ cup frozen peas
4 tablespoons milk (approximately)
15 g (½ oz) butter
2 tablespoons plain flour
pinch of sugar
salt and pepper
½ × 25 g packet potato crisps, crushed
chopped parsley to garnish

Drain the pilchards, reserving the juice. Arrange the pilchards in a shallow ovenproof dish. Cut the egg into quarters and place in the dish. Scatter the celery and peas over the top.

Make the pilchard juice up to ¾ cup with the milk.

Melt the butter in a saucepan and stir in the flour. Cook for 1 minute, then gradually blend in the liquid. Heat, stirring, until the sauce thickens. Add the sugar and salt and pepper to taste.

Pour the sauce over the fish, sprinkle with the crisps and cook in a preheated moderate oven, 180°C (350°F), for 30 minutes.

Garnish with parsley. Serve immediately.

Stuffed Fish Parcels

2 tablespoons parsley and thyme stuffing mix
4 tablespoons boiling water
¼ cup grated Cheddar cheese
salt and pepper
2 fish streaks
knob of butter
SAUCE:
1 tablespoon mayonnaise (see page 73)
1 tablespoon natural low-fat yogurt
1 teaspoon finely chopped parsley
¼ teaspoon dried thyme
TO GARNISH:
watercress sprigs

Place the stuffing mix in a bowl and add the boiling water. Stir in the cheese and salt and pepper to taste.

Place each fish steak on a piece of foil and top with the stuffing. Dot with the butter and fold the foil, enclosing the filling, to make parcels.

Place the parcels on a baking tray and cook in a preheated moderately hot oven, 190°C (375°F), for 20 to 25 minutes. Fold back the foil and continue to cook for 5 to 10 minutes until the topping is golden.

Blend all the sauce ingredients together, with salt and pepper to taste. Transfer the fish to a warmed serving dish. Garnish with watercress and serve the sauce separately.

Potato Fish Bake

300 g (10 oz) fish fillet
½ small onion, finely chopped
3 black peppercorns
1 small dessert apple, peeled, cored and sliced
salt and pepper
¼ teaspoon dried thyme
4 tablespoons dry cider
4-5 tablespoons milk
2 tablespoons plain flour

TOPPING:
½ × 125 g packet instant potato
1 cup boiling water
1 tablespoon milk
knob of butter
grated nutmeg

Place the fish, onion, peppercorns, apple, salt, thyme and cider in a buttered 4 cup ovenproof dish. Cover and cook in a preheated moderate oven, 160°C (325°F), for 20 minutes.

Strain the fish liquor and make up to ¾ cup with the milk. Melt the butter in a saucepan and stir in the flour. Cook for 1 minute, then gradually blend in the fish liquor. Heat, stirring until the sauce thickens. Add salt and pepper to taste.

Flake the fish and add to the sauce with the onion and apple. Heat through gently and transfer to the buttered ovenproof dish.

Make up the potato with the boiling water as directed on the packet. Beat in the milk and butter. Add nutmeg, salt and pepper to taste.

Spread the potato over the fish and mark a pattern on top with a fork. Place under a preheated medium grill for 2 to 3 minutes. Serve immediately.

Salmon Mousse

2 teaspoons gelatine
⅔ cup water
⅔ cup cream
2 eggs, separated
1 teaspoon lemon juice
½ teaspoon anchovy essence (optional)
salt and pepper
1 × 220 g can salmon, drained
TO GARNISH:
cucumber slices
parsley sprigs

Sprinkle the gelatine over the water in a bowl. Place over a saucepan of gently simmering water and stir until dissolved. Cool slightly.

Warm the cream, then beat in the egg yolks. Mix in the dissolved gelatine with the lemon juice, anchovy essence and salt and pepper to taste.

Remove any skin and bones, then mash the salmon until smooth. Add to the egg and cream mixture and mix until thoroughly blended.

Whisk the egg whites until they form soft peaks. Fold into the salmon mixture. Transfer to a 2-3 cup soufflé dish and chill until set.

Serve garnished with cucumber and parsley.

Tuna Pasta Salad

¾ cup pasta shells
salt and pepper
60 g (2 oz) button mushrooms, sliced
½ green pepper, cored, seeded and chopped
½ × 425 g can tomatoes, drained and chopped
1 × 100 g can tuna, drained and flaked
2 teaspoon lemon juice
garlic salt
chopped parsley to garnish

Cook the pasta in plenty of boiling salted water until *al dente* (tender but still firm to the bite). Drain and rinse thoroughly under cold running water.

Place the pasta in a serving bowl and add the mushrooms, green pepper, tomatoes and tuna.

Blend the oil with the lemon juice, then add garlic salt and pepper to taste. Pour the dressing over the pasta and toss well.

Garnish with parsley before serving.

NOTE: The flavour improves if this dish is prepared the day before required and left in the refrigerator overnight.

MEAT & POULTRY

Lamb in Redcurrant and Mint Sauce

2 lamb chops
salt and pepper
30 g (1 oz) butter
1 small onion, sliced
2 tablespoons plain flour
¾ cup stock
2 teaspoons redcurrant jelly
1 teaspoon mint sauce
pinch of sugar
1 tablespoon cream (optional)
mint sprigs to garnish

Trim the chops and sprinkle with salt and pepper. Melt half the butter in a frying pan, add the chops and cook for 10 to 15 minutes on each side. Drain and transfer to a warmed serving dish. Keep hot.

Melt the remaining butter in the pan, add the onion and fry until soft. Stir in the flour and cook for 1 minute. Gradually blend in the stock and heat, stirring, until the sauce thickens.

Add the redcurrant jelly, mint sauce, sugar and salt and pepper to taste. Stir in the cream, if used. Pour the sauce over the chops and garnish with mint.

Serve with new potatoes and peas.

Lamb Hotpot

500 g (1 lb) middle neck of lamb
250 g (8 oz) potatoes, sliced
salt and pepper
1 onion, sliced
2 carrots, sliced
1 celery stick, chopped
½ teaspoon dried mixed herbs
¾ cup stock
15 g (½ oz) butter, melted

Divide the lamb into cutlets.

Cover the base of a 1.2 litre (2 pint) casserole dish with half the potatoes. Arrange the lamb on top and sprinkle liberally with salt and pepper.

Mix together the onion, carrots, celery and herbs, with salt and pepper to taste. Spread over the lamb. Pour over the stock. Arrange the remaining potatoes in overlapping circles on top and brush with the butter.

Cover and cook in a preheated moderate oven, 180°C (350°F), for 1½ hours. Remove the lid and continue to cook for 20 to 30 minutes until the potatoes are browned.

Lamb Parcels

2 lamb chops
salt and pepper
15 g (½ oz) butter
½ × 250 g packet frozen puff pastry, thawed
60 g (2 oz) liver pâté
beaten egg to glaze
watercress sprigs to garnish

Sprinkle the chops with salt and pepper. Melt the butter in a frying pan, add the chops and brown on both sides. Lower the heat and cook for 10 to 15 minutes. Drain on kitchen paper. Cool slightly.

Roll out the pastry to a rectangle about 30 × 15 cm (12 × 6 inches), then cut in half to make two squares.

Spread the chops with the pâté, and place, pâté side down, on the pastry squares. Brush the pastry edges with water. Fold the pastry over the chops and press the edges together to seal. Place on a baking tray, with the seams underneath. Decorate with pastry leaves cut from the trimmings. Brush with egg.

Cook in a preheated hot oven, 220°C (425°F), for 15 minutes. Lower the temperature to moderate, 180°C (350°F), and cook for 15 to 20 minutes.

Transfer to a warmed serving dish and garnish with watercress.

Crispy Sage Lamb

15 g (½ oz) butter
½ onion, chopped
1 tablespoon onion soup powder
⅔ cup milk
375 g (12 oz) cold cooked lamb, chopped
2 tablespoons sage and onion stuffing mix
½ cup boiling water
½ teaspoon dried sage
¼ cup grated Cheddar cheese
salt and pepper
1 tomato, sliced, to garnish

Melt the butter in a saucepan, add the onion and fry until soft. Stir in the soup powder, then gradually blend in the milk. Heat, stirring, until the sauce thickens. Add the lamb and cook until heated through.

Make up the stuffing with the boiling water as directed on the packet. Stir in the sage, cheese and salt and pepper to taste.

Place the lamb in a warmed, greased 3 cup ovenproof dish. Spoon the stuffing over the top and place under a preheated hot grill until the topping is crisp and brown.

Garnish with tomato slices. Serve immediately.

Beef with Orange

1 tablespoon plain flour
salt and pepper
375 g (12 oz) chuck steak, cubed
15 g (½ oz) butter
1 small onion, chopped
½ green pepper, cored, seeded and chopped
grated rind and juice of 1 small orange
¾ cup beef stock
2 tablespoons orange cordial
chopped parsley to garnish

Season the flour with salt and pepper and use to coat the meat. Melt the butter in a pan, add the onion and pepper and fry until soft. Add the meat and fry, turning, until evenly browned. Transfer to a 4 cup casserole dish.

Stir in the orange rind and juice, stock and orange cordial, with salt and pepper to taste. Cover and cook in a preheated moderate oven, 160°C (325°F), for 1 to 1¼ hours.

Serve hot, garnished with parsley.

Beef Crumble

250 g (8 oz) minced beef
1 small onion, finely chopped
1 celery stick, chopped
30 g (1 oz) mushrooms, chopped
1 small carrot, grated
1 teaspoon plain flour
2/3 cup beef stock
1/2 teaspoon Worcestershire sauce
salt and pepper

TOPPING:
3/4 cup wholemeal flour
1/3 cup rolled oats
30 g (1 oz) butter
1/3 cup grated Cheddar cheese
1/2 teaspoon dried mixed herbs

TO GARNISH:
parsley sprigs

Place a frying pan over moderate heat. Add the minced beef and fry in its own fat, turning, until evenly browned. Add the onion, celery, mushrooms and carrot and fry for 5 minutes. Stir in the flour and cook for 1 minute. Add the stock, Worcestershire sauce and salt and pepper to taste. Bring to the boil, stirring. Cover and simmer for 30 to 40 minutes.

To make the topping: Place the flour and oats in a bowl. Rub in the butter until the mixture resembles coarse breadcrumbs. Stir in the cheese, herbs and salt and pepper to taste.

Transfer the meat to a greased 3 cup ovenproof dish and spoon the topping over. Cook in a preheated moderately hot oven, 190°C (375°F) for 20 to 30 minutes.

Serve hot, garnished with parsley.

Chilli Beef

1/3 cup dried red kidney beans
375 g (12 oz) minced beef
1 onion, finely chopped
1/2 small green pepper, cored, seeded and chopped
1/2 × 425 g can tomatoes
2 tablespoons water
1/2-1 teaspoon chilli powder
1/2 teaspoon cumin seeds
salt and pepper

Place the beans in a bowl and cover with cold water. Leave to soak overnight then drain, rinse and place in a saucepan. Cover with fresh cold water. Bring to the boil, simmer for 25 minutes, then drain.

Place a frying pan over moderate heat. Add the minced beef and fry in its own fat, turning, until evenly browned. Add the onion and pepper and fry for 5 minutes. Stir in the tomatoes with their juice, water, chilli powder, cumin and salt and pepper to taste.

Bring to the boil, stirring, then add the beans. Cover and simmer for 1 hour.

Spoon into 2 hot serving bowls. Serve hot, with a green salad and Arab bread, if liked.

Hamburgers with Barbecue Sauce

250 g (8 oz) lean minced beef
2 teaspoons finely chopped onion
½ teaspoon made mustard
2 teaspoons chopped parsley
salt and pepper
15 g (½ oz) butter, melted
SAUCE:
15 g (½ oz) butter
1 onion, finely chopped
1 tablespoon tomato ketchup or sauce
1 tablespoon vinegar
3 teaspoons brown sugar
pinch of chilli powder
½ teaspoon dry mustard
½ teaspoon dried mixed herbs
6 tablespoons water

Place the minced beef, onion, mustard and parsley in a bowl. Add salt and pepper to taste and mix well. Divide the mixture into 4 and shape each piece into a flat cake.

To make the sauce: Melt the butter in a small saucepan, add the onion and fry until soft. Combine the remaining ingredients, mix thoroughly, then add to the pan. Bring to the boil, cover and simmer for 20 minutes.

Brush the hamburgers with the melted butter and cook under a preheated hot grill for 8 to 10 minutes, turning once.

Transfer to a warmed serving dish. Serve hot, with French fried potatoes and green beans or peas. Hand the sauce separately.

Devonshire Pork Casserole

15 g (½ oz) lard
1 small onion, sliced
1 clove garlic, crushed
375 g (12 oz) pork fillet, cubed
2 teaspoons plain flour
½ cup cider
3 tablespoons stock
½ teaspoon dried sage
salt and pepper
1 small cooking apple, peeled, cored and sliced into rings
2 tablespoons cream

Melt the lard in a pan, add the onion and garlic and fry until soft. Add the pork and fry, turning, until evenly browned. Transfer the pork and onion to a 5 cup casserole dish, using a slotted spoon.

Add the flour to the fat remaining in the pan and cook for 1 minute. Gradually blend in the cider and stock and heat, stirring, until the sauce thickens.

Stir in the sage and salt and pepper to taste. Arrange the apple slices in the casserole dish and pour over the sauce. Cover and cook in a preheated moderate oven, 180°C (350°F), for 1½ hours.

Add the cream and serve immediately.

Pork with Prunes

6 prunes
1 teaspoon lemon juice
1 tablespoon plain flour
salt and pepper
2 pork chops, boned
15 g (½ oz) butter
1 teaspoon oil
⅔ cup dry cider or white wine
2 teaspoons redcurrant jelly
3 tablespoons cream
chopped parsley to garnish

Place the prunes in a bowl and cover with cold water. Add the lemon juice and leave to soak overnight.

Season the flour with salt and pepper and use to coat the meat. Heat the butter and oil in a flameproof casserole. Add the chops and fry for 5 minutes on each side. Add the cider or wine, cover and simmer for 30 minutes or until the pork is tender.

Cook the prunes in the soaking liquid for 10 minutes or until tender.

Transfer the meat and prunes to a warmed serving dish, using a slotted spoon; keep hot. Add 3 tablespoons of the prune liquid to the casserole. Stir well and simmer until the sauce is reduced and thickened.

Stir in the redcurrant jelly and cream. Heat gently, then pour over the pork. Garnish with parsley and serve immediately.

Pork with Orange and Apricots

15 g (½ oz) butter
2 pork chops
grated rind and juice of ½ orange
salt and pepper
1 small onion, finely chopped
½ green pepper, cored, seeded and chopped
¾ cup stock
1 teaspoon cornflour
pinch of sugar
½ cup dried apricots
watercress sprigs to garnish

Melt the butter in a frying pan. Add the chops and fry on both sides until evenly browned.

Transfer to a shallow ovenproof dish, using a slotted spoon. Sprinkle with the orange rind and salt and pepper to taste.

Add the onion and pepper to the fat remaining in the pan and fry until soft. Stir in the stock. Blend the cornflour with the orange juice and add to the pan. Heat, stirring, until the sauce thickens. Add the sugar and salt and pepper to taste.

Arrange the apricots on top of the pork and pour over the sauce. Cover with foil and cook in a preheated moderate oven, 180°C (350°F), for 1 to 1¼ hours.

Serve hot, garnished with watercress.

Honey and Apricot Ham

½ cup dried apricots
½ teaspoon made mustard
1 teaspoon honey
salt and pepper
2 ham steaks
2 teaspoons cornflour
½ chicken stock cube, crumbled
parsley sprigs to garnish

Place the apricots in a bowl and cover with cold water. Leave to soak for 2 to 3 hours.

Mix together the mustard, honey and pepper to taste. Spread this mixture over both sides of the ham steaks. Cook under a preheated medium grill for 6 to 8 minutes on each side.

Drain the apricots, reserving the liquid; make this up to ⅔ cup with water if necessary. Blend the cornflour with a little of the liquid, then stir in the remainder.

Pour into a saucepan and heat, stirring, until the sauce thickens. Add the stock cube and apricots and simmer for 1 minute. Check the seasoning.

Place the ham steaks on a warmed serving dish and pour over the sauce. Garnish with parsley. Serve immediately.

Sausage and Black-Eyed Bean Casserole

½ cup black-eyed beans
6 large pork sausages
1 small onion, finely chopped
½ × 425 g can tomatoes
4 tablespoons water
½ beef stock cube, crumbled
½ teaspoon dried mixed herbs
salt and pepper

Place the beans in a bowl, cover with cold water and leave to soak overnight. Drain, rinse and place the beans in a saucepan. Cover with fresh cold water, bring to the boil and simmer for 45 minutes or until tender. Drain.

Cook the sausages under a preheated medium grill, turning frequently, until evenly browned. Cool slightly, then cut into 1 cm (½ inch) pieces. Place in a 5 cup casserole dish.

Add the beans, onion, tomatoes with their juice, water, stock cube, herbs and salt and pepper to taste. Mix well. Cover and cook in a preheated moderate oven, 180°C (350°F) for 45 minutes.

Serve hot, with jacket potatoes.

Italian Veal Casserole

1 tablespoon oil
375 g (12 oz) lean veal, cubed
1 clove garlic, crushed
1 small onion, sliced
½ green pepper, cored, seeded and chopped
125 g (4 oz) tomatoes, skinned and chopped
¾ cup light stock
salt and pepper
1 bouquet garni
chopped parsley to garnish

Heat the oil in a frying pan, add the veal and fry, turning, until golden brown all over. Add the garlic and onion and cook until they are soft.

Stir in the green pepper, tomatoes, stock and salt and pepper to taste. Transfer to a 5 cup casserole dish. Add the bouquet garni. Cover and cook in a preheated moderate oven, 180°C (350°F), for 1 to 1½ hours.

Remove the bouquet garni and skim off any excess fat. Serve hot, garnished with parsley.

Veal Schnitzels

2 × 150 g (5 oz) veal schnitzels
15 g (½ oz) butter
1 teaspoon oil
½ small onion, sliced
60 g (2 oz) button mushrooms
2 tablespoons dry sherry
3 tablespoons cream
salt and pepper
paprika
TO GARNISH:
2 lemon twists
1 teaspoon chopped parsley

Trim the schnitzels into neat shapes and snip the edges to prevent the meat from curling up.

Heat the butter and oil in a frying pan, add the onion and fry for 2 to 3 minutes. Add the veal and mushrooms and cook for 5 to 8 minutes, turning the schnitzels once, until golden brown on both sides.

Stir in the sherry and bring to the boil. Add the cream and heat through, stirring. Add salt and pepper to taste.

Lift the veal schnitzels onto a warmed serving dish and spoon the sauce over. Sprinkle with paprika to taste. Garnish each schnitzel with a lemon twist and chopped parsley.

Piquant Liver

15 g (½ oz) butter
1 small onion, chopped
60 g (2 oz) streaky bacon, derinded and chopped
2 tablespoons plain flour
salt and pepper
300 g (10 oz) lambs' liver, sliced
50 g (2 oz) mushrooms
¾ cup stock
1 tablespoon tomato paste
¼ teaspoon made mustard
2 teaspoons chutney
½ teaspoon sugar
chopped parsley to garnish

Melt the butter in a heavy-based pan, add the onion and bacon and fry until soft.

Season the flour with salt and pepper and use to coat the liver. Add to the pan and fry, turning, until evenly browned. Stir in the mushrooms, stock, tomato paste, mustard, chutney and sugar. Add salt and pepper to taste. Bring to the boil, stirring, then cover and simmer for 20 minutes.

Transfer to a warmed serving dish and garnish with parsley. Serve immediately.

Creamed Kidneys with Salami

4-5 lambs' kidneys
15 g (½ oz) butter
1 small onion, chopped
30 g (1 oz) mushrooms, chopped
2 teaspoons plain flour
⅔ cup stock
1-2 tablespoons raisins
2 slices salami, chopped
salt and pepper
2 tablespoons cream

Remove the skin and core from the kidneys and chop. Melt the butter in a heavy-based pan. Add the onion and fry until soft. Add the kidneys and mushrooms and cook for 2 to 3 minutes. Stir in the flour and cook for 1 minute. Gradually blend in the stock and heat, stirring, until thickened.

Add the raisins, salami and salt and pepper to taste. Cover and simmer for 15 minutes.

Remove from the heat, stir in the cream and serve immediately, with boiled rice.

Celery and Orange Stuffed Hearts

2 lambs' hearts
1 onion, sliced
1 celery stick, chopped
15 g (½ oz) butter
⅔ cup beef stock
STUFFING:
1 cup fresh white breadcrumbs
½ celery stick, finely chopped
grated rind of ½ orange
½ teaspoon dried thyme
salt and pepper
little beaten egg

Remove the fat from the hearts, rinse thoroughly, then drain. Cut out the tubes with scissors.

To make the stuffing: Mix the breadcrumbs, celery, orange rind and thyme with salt and pepper to taste. Bind the mixture with beaten egg.

Fill the hearts with the stuffing, packing it into the cavities firmly. Sew up the openings with string.

Arrange the onion and celery in a 5 cup casserole dish. Melt the butter in a frying pan, add the hearts and fry, turning, until evenly browned. Transfer to the casserole. Season the stock to taste and pour over the hearts. Cover and cook in a preheated moderate oven, 180°C (350°F), for 1½ hours or until tender.

Remove the string and serve the hearts, with the sauce, straight from the casserole.

Curried Chicken

15 g (½ oz) butter
1 small onion, chopped
½ green pepper, cored, seeded and chopped
1 tablespoon curry powder
2 tablespoons plain flour
1½ cups chicken stock
½ dessert apple, cored and chopped
1 tablespoon desiccated coconut
1 tablespoon sweet chutney
3 tablespoons sultanas
salt and pepper
250 g (8 oz) cooked chicken, chopped
chopped parsley to garnish

Melt the butter in a saucepan, add the onion and pepper and fry until soft. Add the curry powder and flour and continue cooking for 1 minute. Gradually blend in the stock and heat, stirring, until thickened.

Stir in the apple, coconut, chutney, sultanas and salt and pepper to taste. Cover and simmer for 10 minutes. Add the chicken and continue cooking for 20 minutes.

Sprinkle with parsley and serve hot, with boiled rice.

Peanut and Cumin Chicken

1 tablespoon oil
2 chicken portions
1 small onion, sliced
2 teaspoons plain flour
2 teaspoons smooth peanut butter
⅔ cup chicken stock
½ teaspoon cumin seeds
salt and pepper
1 tablespoon peanuts, chopped, to garnish

Heat the oil in a pan, add the chicken and brown on all sides. Drain and transfer to a 5 cup casserole dish.

Fry the onion in the oil remaining in the pan until soft. Stir in the flour and peanut butter and cook for 1 minute. Gradually stir in the stock and bring to the boil. Add the cumin and season liberally with salt and pepper.

Pour the sauce over the chicken. Cover and cook in a preheated moderate oven, 180°C (350°F), for 1 to 1¼ hours.

Serve hot, sprinkled with chopped peanuts.

Chicken Maryland

2 tablespoons plain
  flour
salt and pepper
4 chicken drumsticks
1 small egg, beaten
3 tablespoons fresh
  white bread-
  crumbs, toasted
1 tablespoon oil
30 g (1 oz) butter
ACCOMPANIMENTS:
2 rashers streaky
  bacon, derinded
2 bananas
15 g (½ oz) butter
1 × 300 g can
  sweetcorn kernels
TO GARNISH:
watercress sprigs

Season the flour with salt and pepper and use to coat the drumsticks. Dip into the egg, then coat with the breadcrumbs.

Heat the oil and butter in a frying pan, add the chicken and fry, turning, until golden brown all over. Lower the heat, cover and cook gently for 15 to 20 minutes, turning occasionally, until the chicken is tender.

Halve the bacon rashers, roll up and thread onto a skewer. Cook under a preheated hot grill for about 3 minutes.

Cut the bananas in half lengthways. Melt the butter in a pan, add the bananas and fry gently until golden. Heat the sweetcorn in a saucepan, then drain thoroughly.

Drain the chicken and transfer to a warmed serving dish. Arrange the sweetcorn around the chicken and place the bananas and bacon rolls on top.

Garnish with watercress and serve immediately.

Tangy Chicken Salad

3 tablespoons
  sultanas
250 g (8 oz) cooked
  chicken, chopped
2 sticks celery,
  chopped
½ bunch watercress,
  chopped
juice of ½ orange
⅔ cup mayonnaise
  (see page 73)
salt and pepper
TO GARNISH:
watercress sprigs
orange segments

Place the sultanas in a bowl and cover with warm water. Leave to soak for 2 hours then drain.

Put the chicken in a bowl with the celery, watercress and sultanas.

Mix the orange juice with the mayonnaise and add salt and pepper to taste. Add to the chicken and mix well.

Pile onto a serving dish and garnish with watercress and orange segments. Serve cold with rice and a green salad.

Chicken and Bacon Pie

15 g (½ oz) butter
1 small onion, chopped
½ dessert apple, peeled, cored and chopped
2 tablespoons plain flour
¾ cup chicken stock
½ teaspoon dried thyme
185 g (6 oz) cooked chicken, chopped
60 g (2 oz) cooked bacon, chopped
salt and pepper
SHORTCRUST PASTRY:
1 cup plain flour
pinch of salt
30 g (1 oz) margarine
30 g (1 oz) lard
1 tablespoon cold water
beaten egg to glaze

Melt the butter in a pan, add the onion and apple and fry until soft. Stir in the flour and cook for 1 minute. Gradually blend in the stock and heat, stirring, until thickened. Add the thyme, chicken, bacon and salt and pepper to taste. Transfer to a 3 cup pie dish and place a pie funnel in the centre.

To make the pastry: Sift the flour and salt into a bowl. Rub in the fat until the mixture resembles fine breadcrumbs. Add the water and mix to a firm dough. Knead lightly, then chill for 15 minutes.

Roll out on a floured surface to a circle 3.5 cm (1½ inches) larger all round than the dish. Cut a 2.5 cm (1 inch) strip from the edge and place on the dampened rim of the dish. Brush with water and put the pastry lid in position, making a hole in the centre for the funnel. Seal, trim and flute the edges. Decorate with pastry leaves made from the trimmings.

Brush with egg and cook in a preheated moderately hot oven, 200°C (400°F), for 20 to 30 minutes. Serve hot.

Apple and Cherry Duckling

15 g (½ oz) butter
2 duckling joints
1 small onion, chopped
2 teaspoons plain flour
⅔ cup light stock
2 tablespoons dry cider (optional)
1 tablespoon redcurrant jelly
½ teaspoon sugar
salt and pepper
125 g (4 oz) cooking apples, peeled, cored and chopped
90 g (3 oz) black cherries, stoned

Melt the butter in a large saucepan, add the duckling and fry, turning, until evenly browned. Transfer to a 7 cup casserole dish, using a slotted spoon.

Fry the onion in the fat remaining in the pan, until soft. Stir in the flour and cook for 1 minute. Gradually blend in the stock and cider, if used. Heat, stirring until thickened. Add the redcurrant jelly and sugar. Season liberally with salt and pepper.

Arrange the apple and cherries on the duckling and pour over the sauce. Cover and cook in a preheated moderate oven, 180°C (350°F), for 1¼ to 1½ hours. Serve hot.

Turkey Fricassée

25 g (1 oz) streaky bacon, derinded and chopped
1 small onion, chopped
1 small carrot, grated
1 celery stick, chopped
¾ cup light stock
1 bouquet garni
salt and pepper
½ cup milk (approximately)
15 g (½ oz) butter
2 tablespoons plain flour
grated nutmeg
250 g (8 oz) cooked turkey meat, chopped
1 tablespoon cream
chopped parsley to garnish

Place the bacon, onion, carrot, celery, stock and bouquet garni in a saucepan. Add salt and pepper to taste. Bring to the boil, cover and simmer for 15 minutes.

Strain the stock into a measuring jug and add enough milk to make 1½ cups liquor.

Melt the butter in a clean saucepan, stir in the flour and cook for 1 minute. Gradually blend in the liquor and heat, stirring, until thickened. Add nutmeg, salt and pepper to taste.

Stir in the vegetables and turkey meat. Cover and simmer for 15 minutes. Remove from the heat and stir in the cream.

Transfer to a warmed serving dish and sprinkle with parsley. Serve immediately.

EGG & CHEESE DISHES

Crispy Tuna and Egg

1 × 100 g can tuna, drained and flaked
2 tablespoons canned sweetcorn
2 hard-boiled eggs, chopped
15 g (½ oz) butter
2 tablespoons plain flour
¾ cup milk
½ cup grated Cheddar cheese
2 teaspoons chopped chives
salt and pepper
½ × 25 g packet potato crisps, crushed
chopped chives to garnish

Place the fish in a 2 cup ovenproof dish. Spoon the sweetcorn and egg over the top.

Melt the butter in a saucepan, stir in the flour and cook for 1 minute. Gradually blend in the milk, then heat, stirring, until the sauce thickens. Add the cheese, chives and salt and pepper to taste. Pour over the fish.

Sprinkle the crisps over the top and cook in a preheated moderate oven, 180°C (350°F), for 30 minutes.

Serve hot, garnished with chives.

Farmhouse Omelet

30 g (1 oz) butter
1 onion, diced
1 potato, diced
30 g (1 oz) streaky bacon, derinded and chopped
30 g (1 oz) mushrooms, chopped
2 eggs
2 tablespoons milk
¼ teaspoon dried mixed herbs
salt and pepper
½ cup grated Cheddar cheese
chopped parsley to garnish

Melt the butter in a frying pan, add the onion, potato and bacon and cook gently, turning occasionally, until soft. Add the mushrooms, increase the heat and cook until the vegetables begin to brown.

Beat together the eggs, milk and herbs with salt and pepper to taste. Pour over the vegetables, tilting the pan to spread the mixture evenly. Cook over a moderate heat until the omelet starts to set.

Sprinkle with the cheese and place the frying pan under a preheated hot grill until the cheese is bubbling and golden brown.

Sprinkle with parsley and cut the omelet in half. Lift onto warmed serving plates and serve immediately.

Creamy Onion Quiche

SHORTCRUST
PASTRY:
¾ cup plain flour
pinch of salt
15 g (½ oz)
  margarine
30 g (1 oz) lard
1 tablespoon cold
  water
FILLING:
15 g (½ oz) butter
185 g (6 oz) onions,
  thinly sliced
2 eggs
½ cup cream
salt and pepper
TO GARNISH:
chopped chives

Make and chill the pastry as for Chicken and Bacon Pie (see page 43). Roll out and use to line a 15 cm (6 inch) flan dish.

For the filling: Melt the butter in a small frying pan, add the onions and fry until soft. Arrange in the pastry case. Beat together the eggs and cream with salt and pepper to taste. Pour over the onions.

Cook in a preheated moderately hot oven, 200°C (400°F), for 25 to 35 minutes or until the filling is set.

Serve hot or cold, garnished with chives.

2 to 3 servings

Bean and Egg Curry

½ cup haricot beans
15 g (½ oz) butter
2 rashers streaky
  bacon, derinded
  and chopped
1 onion, chopped
1 celery stick,
  chopped
½-1 teaspoon curry
  powder
¼ teaspoon ground
  ginger
1 tablespoon plain
  flour
¾ cup light stock
½ × 425 g can
  tomatoes
salt and pepper
4 hard-boiled eggs
chopped parsley to
  garnish

Place the beans in a bowl, cover with cold water and leave to soak overnight.

Drain, rinse and place in a saucepan. Cover with fresh cold water, bring to the boil and simmer for 45 minutes or until tender, then drain.

Melt the butter in a saucepan, add the bacon, onion and celery and fry until soft. Add the curry powder, ginger and flour and continue to cook for 1 minute. Gradually blend in the stock and the tomatoes with their juice. Heat, stirring until thickened. Add the beans and salt and pepper to taste.

Cut the eggs in half lengthways and add to the curry. Cover and simmer for about 20 minutes. Transfer to a warmed serving dish and garnish with parsley. Serve immediately.

Savoury Cheese Bake

2 slices bread
15 g (½ oz) butter
2 slices cooked ham, chopped
2 tablespoons cooked peas
1 egg, beaten
⅔ cup milk
½ teaspoon made mustard
salt and pepper
½ cup grated mature Cheddar cheese
tomato slices to garnish

Spread the bread with the butter and cut into triangles. Arrange in the base of a greased 2 cup ovenproof dish. Top with the ham and peas.

Beat together the egg, milk, mustard and salt and pepper to taste. Pour into the dish and sprinkle the cheese on top. Cook in a preheated moderately hot oven, 190°C (375°F), for 20 to 25 minutes or until golden and well risen.

Garnish with tomato slices. Serve immediately.

Cheese Fondue Anglais

1 small clove garlic, halved
15 g (½ oz) butter
4 tablespoons dry cider
1 cup grated mature Cheddar cheese
125 g (4 oz) Lancashire cheese, crumbled
1 teaspoon cornflour
1 tablespoon brandy
pepper
grated nutmeg
cubes of crusty bread to serve

Rub the inside of a fondue dish, flameproof casserole or saucepan with the cut garlic clove. Add the butter and cider and heat gently. Add the cheeses and cook gently, stirring, until melted.

Blend the cornflour and brandy to a smooth paste. Add pepper and nutmeg to taste and stir into the fondue. Continue to cook for 3 to 4 minutes until smooth and creamy.

To serve: Keep the fondue warm at the table, preferably over a spirit burner. Place the bread on a serving plate. Each person then spears a piece of bread onto a long-handled fondue fork and dips it into the fondue. Serve accompanied by a green salad.

Scone Pizzas

1 cup self-raising flour
pinch of dry mustard
salt and pepper
30 g (1 oz) margarine
3 tablespoons milk
TOPPING:
1 × 425 g can tomatoes, drained and chopped
2 teaspoons grated onion
¼ teaspoons dried oregano
¼ teaspoon dried basil
2 slices salami, chopped
1 cup grated Cheddar cheese
6 stuffed olives, sliced

Sift the flour with the mustard, a pinch of salt and pepper to taste into a bowl. Rub in the margarine until the mixture resembles fine breadcrumbs. Stir in the milk and mix to a firm dough. Turn onto a floured surface and knead until smooth.

. Divide the dough in half. Roll each piece out to a 15 to 18 cm (6 to 7 inch) circle and place on a large greased baking sheet.

Arrange the tomatoes on top and sprinkle with the onion, herbs and salt and pepper to taste. Sprinkle the salami and cheese over the pizza and top with the olives.

Cook in a preheated moderately hot oven, 200°C (400°F), for 15 to 20 minutes or until the dough is cooked and the cheese is brown and bubbling. Serve warm, with a mixed salad.

Cheese-Topped Savouries

15 g (½ oz) butter
2 rashers streaky bacon, derinded and chopped
60 g (2 oz) mushrooms, sliced
2 tomatoes, skinned and chopped
½ teaspoon made mustard
salt and pepper
4 slices bread, buttered
60 g (2 oz) Cheddar cheese, sliced
parley sprigs to garnish

Melt the butter in a pan, add the bacon and fry until soft. Add the mushrooms and tomatoes and cook for 1 minute. Stir in the mustard and salt and pepper to taste.

Divide the mixture between 2 of the bread slices and top with the remaining 2 slices. Toast both sides under a preheated hot grill until golden brown.

Place the cheese on top and return to the grill. Cook until the cheese is golden and bubbling.

Garnish with parsley. Serve immediately.

Vegetarian Pasties

SHORTCRUST PASTRY:
1 cup plain flour
pinch of salt
30 g (1 oz) margarine
30 g (1 oz) lard
1 tablespoon cold water

FILLING:
90 g (3 oz) mixed vegetables, cooked
1 tablespoon baked beans
60 g (2 oz) Cheddar cheese, diced
1 tablespoon chutney
1 egg yolk, beaten
salt and pepper
milk to glaze
parsley sprigs to garnish

Make and chill the pastry as for Chicken and Bacon Pie (see page 43). Divide in half and roll each piece to a 15 cm (6 inch) circle.

Mix together the vegetables, beans, cheese, chutney, most of the egg yolk and salt and pepper to taste. Divide between the pastry circles, leaving a 1 cm (½ inch) border at the edges.

Add a little milk to the remaining egg yolk and use to brush the pastry edges. Fold the pastry in half, enclosing the filling, and press the edges together. Place on a baking sheet.

Make slits in the top and brush the pasties with the remaining egg and milk. Cook in a preheated moderately hot oven, 190°C (375°F), for 20 to 25 minutes.

Serve hot or cold, garnished with parsley.

Cottage Cheese and Spinach Flan

SHORTCRUST PASTRY:
3/4 cup plain flour
pinch of salt
15 g (1/2 oz) margarine
30 g (1 oz) lard
1 tablespoon cold water

FILLING:
125 g (4 oz) frozen chopped spinach, thawed
salt and pepper
125 g (4 oz) cottage cheese, sieved
1 egg, beaten
2 tablespoons sour cream
grated nutmeg
1/4 cup grated Cheddar cheese

Make and chill the pastry as for Chicken and Bacon Pie (see page 43). Roll out and use to line a 15 cm (6 inch) flan dish or tin, standing on a baking sheet.

Drain the spinach thoroughly and place in the pastry case. Sprinkle with salt and pepper.

Mix together the cottage cheese, egg, sour cream and salt, pepper and nutmeg to taste. Pour over the spinach and sprinkle with the grated cheese.

Cook in a preheated moderately hot oven, 200°C (400°F), for 25 to 35 minutes or until the filling is set. Serve hot or cold.

2 to 3 servings

Cheese Pots

45 g (1½ oz) blue vein cheese
30 g (1 oz) butter, softened
½ cup finely grated Cheddar cheese
2 tablespoons milk
1 small clove garlic, crushed
1 teaspoon chopped chives
salt and pepper
parsley sprigs to garnish

Place the blue vein and butter in a bowl and beat until thoroughly blended. Beat in the Cheddar cheese and milk. Add the garlic, chives and salt and pepper to taste.

Divide the mixture between 2 small serving pots or dishes and chill before serving. Garnish with parsley and serve with hot toast.

Cheese Medley Coleslaw

125 g (4 oz) white cabbage, finely shredded
1 carrot, grated
1 celery stick, chopped
30 g (1 oz) Edam cheese, diced
30 g (1 oz) Double Gloucester cheese, diced
30 g (1 oz) Danish blue cheese, diced
2 tablespoons natural low-fat yogurt
2 tablespoons mayonnaise (see page 73)
salt and pepper
chopped parsley to garnish

Place the vegetables and cheeses in a serving bowl and mix together.

Combine the yogurt and mayonnaise with salt and pepper to taste. Pour over the salad and toss well.

Sprinkle with parsley. Serve with crusty rolls and butter.

VEGETABLES & SALADS

Cheesy Cauliflower

1 small cauliflower, divided into florets
salt and pepper
15 g (½ oz) butter
2 tablespoons plain flour
¾ cup milk
45 g (1½ oz) Danish blue cheese, crumbled
1 tablespoon dry breadcrumbs

Cook the cauliflower in boiling salted water for about 12 minutes until tender. Drain and transfer to a warmed ovenproof serving dish.

Melt the butter in a saucepan, stir in the flour and continue cooking for 1 minute. Gradually blend in the milk and heat, stirring, until thickened.

Stir in the cheese and heat gently, stirring, until melted. Add salt and pepper to taste.

Pour the sauce over the cauliflower and top with the breadcrumbs. Place under a preheated medium grill until the topping is golden brown. Serve hot.

Caraway Cabbage

375 g (12 oz) red or white cabbage, shredded
1 small onion, chopped
½ teaspoon caraway seeds
salt and pepper
15 g (½ oz) butter
½ red pepper, cored, seeded and sliced

Place the cabbage, onion and caraway seeds in a pan of boiling salted water. Cook for 5 to 10 minutes, drain and return to the pan.

Add the butter and red pepper and toss the ingredients over a low heat for 1 minute. Add salt and pepper to taste and transfer to a warmed serving dish. Serve immediately.

Vegetarian Hotpot

¼ cup dried chick peas
¼ cup dried haricot beans
¼ cups dried black-eyed beans
¼ cups dried red kidney beans
15 g (½ oz) butter
1 small onion, chopped
1 carrot, sliced
1 celery stick, chopped
1 clove garlic, crushed
½ × 425 g can tomatoes
½ teaspoon dried mixed herbs
salt and pepper
¾ cup grated Cheddar cheese

Place the chick peas, haricot beans and black-eyed beans in a bowl and cover with cold water. Place the kidney beans in a separate bowl and cover with water. Leave to soak overnight.

Drain and place the chick peas, haricot beans and black-eyed beans in a saucepan; put the kidney beans in a separate pan (to avoid tinting the others pink). Cover the beans with fresh cold water. Bring to the boil, cover and simmer for 40 minutes or until tender. Drain, rinse under cold water, then drain thoroughly.

Melt the butter in a saucepan, add the onion, carrot and celery and fry until soft. Stir in the garlic, beans, tomatoes with their juice, herbs and salt and pepper to taste.

Bring to the boil, cover and simmer for 1 to 1¼ hours, adding a little water if the mixture becomes too dry. Check the seasoning. Transfer to a warmed serving dish. Sprinkle with the cheese. Serve immediately.

Spiced Vegetables and Rice

1 tablespoon oil
1 leek, sliced
1 carrot, thinly sliced
1 onion, sliced
½ dessert apple, cored and chopped
½ teaspoon cumin seeds
½ teaspoon ground coriander
pinch of cayenne pepper
salt and pepper
4-5 tablespoons stock
½ cup brown rice
chopped parsley to garnish

Heat the oil in a saucepan, add the leek, carrot, onion and apple and cook gently, stirring, for 3 minutes. Add the cumin, coriander, cayenne and salt and pepper to taste. Continue to cook for 3 minutes, then stir in the stock. Cover and simmer for 10 to 15 minutes until the vegetables are tender but not soft.

Cook the rice in plenty of boiling salted water for 45 to 50 minutes or until tender. Drain and rinse with boiling water.

Stir the rice into the vegetables and heat gently for 5 minutes. Transfer to a warmed serving dish and garnish with parsley. Serve hot.

Mediterranean Vegetables

1 small eggplant
salt and pepper
1 tablespoon oil
1 small onion, sliced
1 small clove garlic, crushed
1 celery stick, chopped
½ green pepper, cored, seeded and chopped
2 tomatoes, skinned and chopped
2 tablespoons water
½ teaspoon dried oregano
½ teaspoon dried basil
chopped parsley to garnish

Cut the eggplant into thin slices and sprinkle with salt. Place in a colander and leave for 30 minutes. Rinse and pat dry with kitchen paper.

Heat the oil in a saucepan and add the eggplant, onion, garlic, celery and green pepper. Cook, stirring, until all the vegetables are coated with oil. Cover and cook for 10 minutes.

Add the tomatoes, water, oregano, basil and salt and pepper to taste. Bring to the boil, cover and simmer for 30 minutes.

Serve hot or cold, sprinkled with parsley.

Minted Zucchini with Peas and Corn

175 g (6 oz) zucchini, thinly sliced
salt
60 g (2 oz) frozen peas
60 g (2 oz) frozen sweetcorn
2 mint sprigs
15 g (½ oz) butter
2 teaspoons chopped chives

Place the zucchini in a pan of boiling salted water. Add the peas, sweetcorn and mint. Cover and simmer for 3 to 4 minutes until the vegetables are just tender. Drain, remove the mint and return the vegetables to the pan.

Add the butter and chives and toss over a low heat for 1 minute. Transfer to a warmed serving dish. Serve hot.

Peas French-Style

1 × 250 g packet frozen peas
3 lettuce leaves, shredded
30 g (1 oz) butter
3 spring onions, finely chopped
½ teaspoon sugar
4 tablespoons light stock
1 sprig each parsley and mint, tied together
salt and pepper

Place all the ingredients in a saucepan, adding salt and pepper to taste. Bring slowly to the boil, cover and simmer for 15 to 20 minutes or until the peas are tender, adding more stock or water if necessary.

Discard the parsley and mint. Transfer to a serving dish. Serve immediately.

Layered Potatoes with Sour Cream

375 g (12 oz)
  potatoes, thinly
  sliced
1 small onion, finely
  chopped
4 tablespoons sour
  cream
salt and pepper
45 g (1½ oz) butter
4 tablespoons milk
chopped chives to
  garnish

Line the base of a greased 3 cup ovenproof dish with potato slices. Add a little of the onion and sour cream. Sprinkle liberally with salt and pepper. Repeat the layers until all these ingredients are used, finishing with a layer of potato.

Melt 30 g (1 oz) of the butter in a saucepan, stir in the milk and pour over the potatoes. Dot the remaining butter on top.

Cover and cook in a preheated moderately hot oven, 190°C (375°F), for 45 minutes. Uncover and cook for a further 20 minutes or until the potatoes are golden brown.

Garnish with chives. Serve hot with lamb chops or sausages and bacon.

Baked Zucchini

15 g (½ oz) butter
1 small onion, chopped
250 g (8 oz) zucchini, sliced
1 large tomato, skinned and sliced
½ teaspoon dried oregano
salt and pepper
1 egg, beaten
½ cup grated Gruyère cheese
parsley sprigs to garnish

Melt the butter in a saucepan, add the onion and zucchini and fry for 2 minutes. Transfer to a shallow ovenproof dish and place the tomato slices on top. Sprinkle with the oregano and salt and pepper to taste.

Mix together the egg, cheese and salt and pepper to taste. Spoon over the tomato. Cook in a preheated moderate oven, 180°C (350°F), for 15 to 20 minutes until the topping is golden.

Garnish with parsley. Serve hot.

Savory Stuffed Peppers

2 medium green peppers
salt and pepper
15 g (½ oz) butter
½ small onion, finely chopped
2 rashers streaky bacon, derinded and chopped
½ cup long-grain rice, cooked
½ cup grated Cheddar cheese
4 tablespoons cream
¼ teaspoon made mustard
1 teaspoon chopped parsley

Cut the tops from the peppers and reserve; discard the seeds and cores. Blanch in boiling salted water for 2 minutes, remove and drain.

Melt the butter in a saucepan, add the onion and bacon and fry until soft. Remove from the heat and stir in the cooked rice and cheese.

Beat the cream with the mustard, parsley and salt and pepper to taste, then stir into the rice mixture. Pile this mixture into the pepper shells. Replace the tops.

Place in a shallow ovenproof dish, cover with foil and cook in a preheated moderate oven, 180°C (350°F), for 15 to 20 minutes. Serve hot.

Bean Sprout Salad

125 g (4 oz) fresh bean sprouts
1 celery stick, chopped
1 carrot, grated
2.5 cm (1 inch) piece of cucumber, cut in strips
3 tablespoons raisins
1 tablespoon French dressing (see page 73)
1 tablespoon natural low-fat yogurt
salt and pepper

Place the bean sprouts, celery, carrot, cucumber and raisins in a bowl.

Combine the French dressing with the yogurt. Season with salt and pepper to taste. Pour over the salad and toss well. Serve with meat or fish.

Onion and Avocado Salad

60 g (2 oz) streaky bacon, derinded
½ avocado
2 teaspoons lemon juice
3 crisp lettuce leaves, shredded
2 spring onions, chopped
2 tablespoons salted peanuts
2 tablespoons French dressing (see page 73)
salt and pepper

Cook the bacon under a preheated medium grill until crisp. Chop into small pieces and leave to cool.

Peel, stone and slice the avocado. Place in a serving bowl and sprinkle with the lemon juice. Add the lettuce, spring onions, bacon, peanuts and French dressing. Toss well and season with salt and pepper to taste. Chill before serving.

Fruit Coleslaw

- 1 red-skinned dessert apple, cored and chopped
- 2 teaspoons lemon juice
- 125 g (4 oz) white cabbage, finely shredded
- 1 small carrot, grated
- 1/3 cup dates, stoned and chopped
- 1 tablespoon sultanas
- 60 g (2 oz) green grapes, halved and seeded
- 2 tablespoons natural low-fat yogurt
- 2 tablespoons mayonnaise (see page 73)
- salt and pepper

Place the apple in a bowl, sprinkle with the lemon juice and toss well. Add the cabbage, carrot, dates, sultanas and grapes.

Mix together the yogurt, mayonnaise and salt and pepper to taste. Pour over the salad and toss well. Pile into a serving dish.

Cheese-Filled Avocado

1 avocado
1 teaspoon lemon juice
60 g (2 oz) Danish blue cheese
2 tablespoons cottage cheese
salt and pepper
parsley sprigs to garnish

Halve the avocado, remove the stone and scoop out some of the flesh, leaving 1 cm (½ inch) thick shells. Reserve the shells.

Place the avocado flesh and lemon juice in a bowl and mash, using a fork. Blend in the cheeses and salt and pepper to taste.

Pile the mixture into the avocado shells. Serve chilled, garnished with parsley.

Orange Pasta Salad

3/4 cup pasta shells
salt and pepper
1/2 cup canned red
  kidney beans,
  drained
1/2 green pepper,
  cored, seeded and
  chopped
2 teaspoons chopped
  parsley
grated rind and juice
  of 1/2 orange
1 tablespoon French
  dressing (see page
  73)

Cook the pasta in plenty of boiling salted water until just tender. Drain and rinse under cold running water.

Place the pasta in a serving bowl. Add the kidney beans, pepper, parsley and orange rind. Mix the orange juice with the French dressing and add salt and pepper to taste. Pour over the salad and toss well. Chill before serving.

Creamy Potato Salad

250 g (8 oz) boiled
  potatoes, diced
few watercress sprigs,
  chopped
30 g (1 oz) cooked
  ham, chopped
4 tablespoons cream
1 teaspoon made
  mustard
pinch of sugar
salt and pepper
watercress sprigs to
  garnish

Place the potatoes (preferably while still warm) in a bowl and add the chopped watercress and ham.

Lightly whip the cream with the mustard, sugar and salt and pepper to taste. Add to the potatoes and mix well.

Pile into a serving dish. Leave in a cool place for at least 30 minutes before serving to allow the potatoes to absorb the dressing.

Garnish with watercress and serve with cold meats.

Apple and Nut Salad

2 dessert apples, cored and chopped
2 teaspoons lemon juice
2 celery sticks, chopped
2 tablespoons salted peanuts
¼ cup chopped walnuts
3 tablespoons mayonnaise (see page 73)
few lettuce leaves
paprika to garnish

Place the apples in a bowl, sprinkle with lemon juice and toss well. Add the remaining ingredients, except the lettuce; mix well.

Line a serving dish with lettuce leaves, pile the salad on top and sprinkle with paprika to garnish.

French Dressing

3 teaspoons French mustard
½ teaspoon sugar
1 teaspoon each finely chopped chives and parsley
4 tablespoons vinegar
8 tablespoons salad or olive oil
salt and pepper

Mix together the mustard, sugar and herbs. Stir in the vinegar. Transfer to a screw-top jar and add the oil and salt and pepper to taste. Shake vigorously to blend before serving.
Makes about 1¼ cups

Mayonnaise

2 egg yolks
½ teaspoon salt
½ teaspoon pepper
½ teaspoon dry mustard
1 teaspoon caster sugar
1¼ cups salad or olive oil
1½ tablespoons white vinegar or lemon juice

Make sure that all the ingredients are at room temperature.

Beat the egg yolks in a bowl with the salt, pepper, mustard and sugar. Add the oil, drop by drop, beating constantly. As the mayonnaise thickens the oil may be added in a thin stream.

When all of the oil has been added, gradually add the vinegar and mix thoroughly.
Makes about 1¼ cups

DESSERTS

Raspberry Soufflé Omelet

4 tablespoons stewed raspberries
4 eggs, separated
2 tablespoons caster sugar
2 tablespoons water
pinch of salt
TO FINISH:
few fresh raspberries
sifted icing sugar

Place the raspberries in a greased shallow ovenproof dish.

Whisk the egg yolks and sugar together until pale. Stir in the water.

Whisk the egg whites with the salt until stiff, then fold into the egg yolks. Pour over the raspberries and cook in a preheated moderate oven, 180°C (350°F), for 15 to 20 minutes.

Top with the raspberries and sprinkle with icing sugar. Serve immediately, with cream.

Gooseberry and Hazelnut Brûlée

250 g (8 oz) gooseberries
¼ cup sugar
⅔ cup hazelnut yogurt
1 tablespoon brown sugar

Place the gooseberries in a saucepan with sugar to taste. Cook gently, stirring, until the juices run, then cover and simmer until tender.

Spoon into individual heatproof dishes and leave to cool. Top with the yogurt and chill well.

Just before serving, sprinkle with brown sugar and place under a preheated hot grill for 1 to 2 minutes. Serve immediately.

Baked Bananas

2 bananas, thickly sliced
2 teaspoons lemon juice
2 tablespoons dates, chopped
2 teaspoons honey
1 tablespoon water
1-2 tablespoons chopped walnuts

Place the bananas in a 2 cup ovenproof dish, add the lemon juice and toss well. Sprinkle the dates over the top.

Blend together the honey and water and spoon over the bananas. Top with the walnuts. Cover with foil and cook in a preheated moderate oven, 180°C (350°F), for 20 minutes. Serve hot, with cream.

Date and Lemon Pudding

3 slices buttered wholemeal bread, crusts removed and quartered
3 tablespoons dates, stoned and chopped
1 egg
2 tablespoons brown sugar
1 teaspoon finely grated lemon rind
¼ teaspoon ground mixed spice
1¼ cups milk

Arrange the bread in a greased 3 cup ovenproof dish. Sprinkle the dates over the top.

Beat together the egg, 1 tablespoon of the sugar, the lemon rind and spice. Heat the milk, but do not boil; stir into the egg mixture.

Strain the custard over the bread and leave for 10 to 15 minutes. Stand the dish in a roasting pan, containing enough water to come halfway up the dish. Cook in a preheated moderate oven, 180°C (350°F), for 25 to 30 minutes or until the custard is just set.

Sprinkle with the remaining sugar and serve immediately.

Spiced Apple Amber

250 g (8 oz) cooking apples, peeled, cored and sliced
2 teaspoons honey
¼ teaspoon ground cinnamon
¼ teaspoon grated nutmeg
1 tablespoon water
1 egg, separated
1 tablespoon caster sugar

Place the apples, honey, cinnamon, nutmeg and water in a saucepan. Heat gently until the apples are tender. Cool slightly, then sieve or purée in an electric blender. Beat in the egg yolk, then spoon into a buttered 3 cup ovenproof dish.

Whisk the egg white until stiff, then whisk in half the sugar. Fold in the remainder and spoon over the apples.

Cook in a preheated moderate oven, 180°C (350°F), for 10 to 15 minutes. Serve hot, with cream.

Banana Splits with Fudge Sauce

2 bananas
4 tablespoons vanilla ice cream
4 tablespoons cream, whipped
2 teaspoons chopped nuts
1 glacé cherry, halved
SAUCE:
15 g ($\frac{1}{2}$ oz) plain chocolate
1 tablespoon warm water
$\frac{1}{3}$ cup brown sugar
1 teaspoon golden syrup
2-3 drops vanilla essence

Cut the bananas in half lengthways and sandwich the halves together with the ice cream. Place on individual serving plates. Spoon or pipe the cream on top and decorate with the nuts and cherry pieces.

To make the sauce: Melt the chocolate with the water in a basin standing over a pan of hot water.

Transfer to a saucepan and add the sugar and syrup. Heat gently, stirring, until the sugar has dissolved. Bring to the boil and boil steadily, without stirring, for 3 to 4 minutes. Remove from the heat and stir in the vanilla.

Pour the sauce over the banana splits or hand separately.

Spicy Orange Creamed Rice

2 tablespoons short-grain rice
$\frac{3}{4}$ cup water
$1\frac{1}{4}$ cups milk
2 tablespoons brown sugar
1 teaspoon finely grated orange rind
$\frac{1}{4}$ teaspoon grated nutmeg
1-2 tablespoons sultanas
1 bay leaf
15 g ($\frac{1}{2}$ oz) butter

Place the rice in a saucepan with the water. Bring to the boil, cover and simmer for 10 minutes. Drain and place the rice in a 3 cup ovenproof dish. Add the remaining ingredients.

Cook in a preheated moderate oven, 160°C (325°F) for 1½ to 2 hours, stirring twice during the first hour to incorporate the skin and increase the creaminess. Serve hot or cold.

Plum Tart

1 cup plain flour
pinch of salt
1 teaspoon caster sugar
90 g (3 oz) butter
1 egg, beaten
FILLING:
250 g (8 oz) red plums, halved and stoned
¾ cup water
¼ cup sugar
2 teaspoons cornflour
TO FINISH:
sifted icing sugar

Sift the flour and salt into a bowl and add the sugar. Rub in the butter until the mixture resembles breadcrumbs. Add the egg and mix to a smooth dough. Knead lightly, cover and chill for 30 minutes.

Roll out the dough on a floured surface and use to line a 15 cm (6 inch) flan ring placed on a baking sheet. Reserve the trimmings.

Put the plums, water and sugar in a saucepan. Cook gently until tender. Drain, reserving the juice.

Blend the cornflour with a little cooled juice, then add the remainder. Bring to the boil, stirring. Add the plums and spoon into the pastry case. Cut strips from the pastry trimmings and make a lattice pattern over the filling.

Cook in a preheated moderately hot oven, 200°C (400°F), for 25 minutes. Cool in the tin.

When cold, transfer to a serving plate and sprinkle with icing sugar.
2 to 3 servings

Banana Orange Caramel

1 banana, sliced
1 pear, peeled, cored and sliced
pinch of ground cinnamon
grated rind and juice of ½ orange
1 tablespoon water
¼ cup sugar
2 eggs, beaten
toasted almonds to decorate

Place the banana, pear, cinnamon, orange rind and juice in a saucepan and simmer for 5 minutes. Remove from the heat and leave to cool.

Place the water and sugar in a saucepan and heat gently until dissolved. Bring to the boil and boil steadily until a rich golden brown caramel is formed. Pour into buttered dariole moulds or individual dishes.

Strain the eggs over the fruit and stir well. Pour into the moulds.

Place in a roasting pan containing enough water to come halfway up the dishes. Cook in a preheated cool oven, 150°C (300°F), for 25 to 30 minutes or until just firm.

Leave in the refrigerator overnight. Just before serving, turn out and sprinkle with almonds. Serve with cream.

Chocolate and Orange Mousse

60 g (2 oz) dark chocolate
knob of butter
grated rind and juice of ½ orange
1 egg, separated
4 tablespoons cream, whipped
chocolate curls to decorate (see note)

Melt the chocolate in a basin over a pan of hot water. Remove from the heat and add the butter, orange rind and juice, and the egg yolk. Beat until smooth. Leave to cool.

Fold in the whipped cream. Whisk the egg white until just firm and fold into the chocolate mixture. Pour into individual serving dishes. Chill in the refrigerator until set.

Decorate with the chocolate curls before serving.

NOTE: To make chocolate curls, shave slivers from a chocolate block, using a potato peeler.

Ginger and Nut Ice Cream

⅔ cup cream
2 tablespoons icing sugar, sifted
2 tablespoons preserved ginger, finely chopped
2 teaspoons ginger syrup
1-2 tablespoons finely chopped hazelnuts

Place the cream in a bowl and whip lightly. Fold in the icing sugar. Pour into a shallow freezer tray, cover and freeze for about 45 minutes, until the ice cream has frozen around the sides of the tray.

Turn into a chilled bowl and whisk until smooth. Stir in the ginger, syrup and hazelnuts.

Return the ice cream to the tray, cover and freeze until firm.

Transfer to the refrigerator about 10 minutes before serving to soften. Scoop into individual dishes. Serve with crisp biscuits if liked.

Melon and Orange with Mint

½ small honeydew melon
1 orange
few mint leaves, crushed
mint sprigs to decorate

Remove the pips from the melon, cut the flesh from the skin and chop into pieces. Place in a bowl.

Grate the rind from the orange and add to the melon. Peel and segment the orange, discarding all the pith. Add to the melon with the crushed mint. Mix well and pile into individual serving dishes. Chill before serving.

Decorate with mint sprigs and serve with cream or ice cream.

Crunchy Apples

250 g (8 oz) cooking apples, peeled, cored and sliced
¼ cup sugar
1 teaspoon lemon juice
1 tablespoon water
¼ teaspoon ground cinnamon
20 g (¾ oz) butter
½ cup rolled oats
1 tablespoon brown sugar
4 tablespoons cream
grated chocolate to decorate

Place the apples in a saucepan with the sugar, lemon juice, water and cinnamon. Cook gently until the fruit is soft. Beat to a pulp with a wooden spoon, then transfer to individual glass serving dishes.

Melt the butter in a saucepan and add the rolled oats and brown sugar. Heat gently, stirring, until the oats are browned; leave to cool. Spoon over the apples.

Whip the cream lightly and spoon over the topping. Decorate with chocolate.

Apricot and Chocolate Dessert

2 thick slices chocolate Swiss roll
4 canned apricot halves
4 tablespoons apricot yogurt
4 tablespoons cream, whipped
grated chocolate to decorate

Place the Swiss roll in individual serving dishes. Drain the apricots and use a little of the juice to moisten the Swiss roll. Chop the apricots and spoon over the Swiss roll.

Fold the yogurt into the cream, spoon over the apricots and decorate with grated chocolate. Serve chilled.

Blackcurrant Syllabub

125 g (4 oz) blackcurrants
1 tablespoon sugar
grated rind and juice of ½ lemon
1 tablespoon sherry
½ cup cream
1 tablespoon caster sugar

Place the blackcurrants, sugar, lemon rind and juice in a saucepan and cook gently for 5 minutes. Cool slightly, then purée in an electric blender or rub through a sieve. Stir in the sherry.

Place the cream, caster sugar and half the blackcurrant purée in a bowl and whisk until the mixture forms soft peaks.

Spoon the remaining purée into the base of 2 glasses and top with the cream mixture. Chill before serving, with sponge fingers if liked.

NOTE: Any soft fruit can be used instead of blackcurrants.

Pineapple Freeze

½ fresh pineapple
1-2 tablespoons water
⅓ cup icing sugar, sifted
mint sprigs to decorate

Cut the flesh from the pineapple, discarding the central core; reserve the shell. Chop and place in an electric blender. Add a little water and work to a purée. Stir in the icing sugar.

Pile the mixture into the reserved shell, cover and freeze until firm.

Transfer to the refrigerator 20 minutes before serving to soften slightly. Decorate with mint sprigs.

Apricot and Banana Cream

½ cup dried apricots
2 ripe bananas
1 teaspoon lemon juice
4 tablespoons cream
2 tablespoons natural low-fat yogurt
2 teaspoons honey
2 walnut halves to decorate

Place the apricots in a bowl and pour over cold water to cover. Leave to soak for a few hours; drain.

Place the bananas in an electric blender with the apricots, lemon juice, cream, yogurt and honey. Blend to a smooth cream.

Spoon into individual glass serving dishes and chill before serving. Decorate with walnut halves.

Coffee Junket

1¼ cups milk
1 teaspoon caster sugar
1 teaspoon instant coffee powder
½ junket tablet dissolved in water
2 walnut pieces to decorate

Place the milk, sugar and coffee in a saucepan. Heat gently, stirring to dissolve the coffee and sugar, until the mixture reaches 36°C (97°F) or 'blood heat'.

Stir in the dissolved junket tablet and pour into individual serving bowls. Leave at room temperature for 1½ hours or until set.

Chill before serving. Decorate with walnut pieces.

Quick Rhubarb Fool

250 g (8 oz) rhubarb, chopped
1 tablespoon water
grated rind of ½ orange
¼ cup sugar
½ cup cream, whipped
3 tablespoons raspberry yogurt

Place the rhubarb in a saucepan with the water, orange rind and sugar. Cook gently until soft. Leave to cool, then purée in an electric blender or rub through a sieve.

Fold two-thirds of the cream into the rhubarb with the yogurt. Spoon into individual glass dishes and pipe whirls of cream on top. Chill before serving.

Orange Cheesecake

30 g (1 oz) butter
60 g (2 oz) Nice biscuits, crushed
FILLING:
125 g (4 oz) cottage cheese
1 tablespoon caster sugar
grated rind and juice of ½ orange
½ cup cream, whipped
mandarin segments to decorate

Melt the butter and stir in the crushed biscuits. Press the mixture onto the base and sides of a 15 cm (6 inch) flan dish. Leave in the refrigerator until firm.

Mix the cottage cheese with the sugar, orange rind and juice. Fold in two-thirds of the cream. Spoon the mixture into the biscuit flan case.

Decorate with the remaining cream and mandarin segments. Chill before serving.
2 to 3 servings

Summer Fruits and Sour Cream Dessert

- 1 tablespoon sugar
- 3 tablespoons water
- 185 g (6 oz) red plums, stoned
- 125 g (4 oz) raspberries
- 4 tablespoons sour cream
- 2 teaspoons brown sugar

Place the sugar and water in a saucepan and heat gently until dissolved. Increase the heat and boil steadily for 2 minutes. Allow to cool, then chill.

Cut the plums into slices. Divide the plums and raspberries between individual serving dishes and pour over the syrup.

Spoon the sour cream over the fruit and sprinkle with brown sugar. Serve chilled.

Apple and Pear Ginger Trifle

1 medium cooking apple, peeled, cored and sliced
1 medium pear, peeled, cored and sliced
4 tablespoons cider
2 tablespoons brown sugar
¼ teaspoon ground ginger
3 slices ginger cake, cut in half
4 tablespoons cream
2 teaspoons icing sugar, sifted
1 tablespoon chopped nuts, toasted

Place the apple and pear in a saucepan with the cider, brown sugar and ginger. Cook gently until the fruit is just tender. Leave to cool.

Arrange the cake in individual glass serving dishes and spoon the fruit and cooking liquid over the top.

Lightly whip the cream and fold in the icing sugar. Spoon over the fruit and sprinkle with the nuts. Serve chilled.

INDEX

Apple:
  Apple and cherry duckling 44
  Apple and nut salad 73
  Apple and pear ginger trifle 93
  Crunchy apples 85
  Spiced apple amber 76
Apricot:
  Apricot and banana cream 89
  Apricot and chocolate dessert 86
  Honey and apricot ham 34
  Pork with orange and apricots 33
Avocado:
  Cheese-filled avocado 69
  Onion and avocado salad 67

Banana:
  Apricot and banana cream 89
  Baked bananas 76
  Banana orange caramel 81
  Banana splits with fudge sauce 79
  Bream with banana with nuts 16
Barbecue sauce, hamburgers with 31
Bean:
  Bean and egg curry 48
  Beany breakfast 10
  Sausage and black-eyed bean casserole 35
Bean sprout salad 66
Beef:
  Beef crumble 29
  Beef with orange 28
  Chilli beef 30
Blackcurrant syllabub 87
Bran yogurt 7
Bream with banana and nuts 16

Caraway cabbage 57
Cauliflower:
  Cheesy cauliflower 56
Celery and orange stuffed hearts 39
Cereal medley 9
Cheese:
  Cheese-filled avocado 69
  Cheese fondue anglais 50
  Cheese medley coleslaw 55
  Cheese pots 54
  Cheese-topped savouries 51
  Cheesy cauliflower 56
  Savoury cheese bake 49
Chicken:
  Chicken and bacon pie 43
  Chicken Maryland 42
  Curried chicken 40
  Peanut and cumin chicken 41
  Tangy chicken salad 42
Chilli beef 30
Chocolate and orange mousse 82
Coffee junket 90
Cottage cheese and spinach flan 53
Curried dishes:
  Bean and egg curry 48
  Curried chicken 40

Date and lemon pudding 76

Egg:
  Bean and egg curry 48
  Crispy tuna and egg 46
  Farmhouse omelet 47
  Onion and tomato scramble 12
  Pilchard and egg supper 20
  Raspberry soufflé omelet 74

Fish. *See also* Bream, etc.
  Crispy tangy fish 19
  Fish with lemon and watercress sauce 16
  Fish with sour cream and mushrooms 15
  Herb fish cakes 17
  Potato fish bake 22
  Stuffed fish parcels 21
Fondue, cheese 50
French dressing 73
Fruit. *See also* Apple, etc.
  Fruit coleslaw 68
  Summer fruit and sour cream dessert 92

Ginger and nut ice cream 83
Gooseberry:
  Gooseberry and hazelnut brûlée 75
  Mullet with gooseberries 14
Grapefruit, tangy 6

Ham, honey and apricot 34
Hamburgers with barbecue sauce 31
Hearts, celery and orange stuffe 39

Herb fish cakes 17
Honey and apricot ham 34

Kidneys, creamed, with salami 38
Kipper toast 10
Kipper vol-au-vent 18

Lamb:
  Crispy sage lamb 27
  Lamb hotpot 25
  Lamb parcels 26
  Lamb in redcurrant and mint sauce 24
Lancashire buns 13
Liver, piquant 38

Mayonnaise 73
Melon and orange with mint 84
Milk and orange nog 10
Muesli 8
Mullet with gooseberries 14

Onion:
  Creamy onion quiche 48
  Onion and avocado salad 67
  Onion and tomato scramble 12
Orange:
  Banana orange caramel 81
  Beef with orange 28
  Milk and orange nog 10
  Orange cheesecake 90
  Orange pasta salad 70
  Spicy orange creamed rice 79

Pasties, vegetarian 52
Peanut and cumin chicken 41
Peas French-style 62
Peppers, savoury stuffed 65
Pilchard and egg supper 20
Pineapple freeze 88
Pizzas, scone 50
Plum tart 80
Pork:
  Devonshire pork casserole 32
  Pork with orange and apricots 33
  Pork with prunes 32

Potato:
  Creamy potato salad 71
  Layered potatoes with sour cream 63
  Potato fish bake 22
Prunes, pork with 32

Raspberry soufflé omelet 74
Rhubarb fool, quick 90
Rice:
  Spiced vegetables and rice 59
  Spicy orange creamed rice 79

Salads:
  Apple and nut salad 73
  Bean sprout salad 66
  Cheese medley coleslaw 55
  Creamy potato salad 71
  Onion and avocado salad 67
  Fruit coleslaw 68
  Orange pasta salad 70
  Tangy chicken salad 42
  Tuna pasta salad 23
Salami, creamed kidneys with 38
Salmon mousse 23
Sausage and black-eyed bean casserole 35
Sausage parcels 13
Scone pizzas 50

Trifle 93
Tuna:
  Crispy tuna and egg 46
  Tuna pasta salad 23
Turkey fricassée 45

Veal:
  Italian veal casserole 36
  Veal schnitzels 37
Vegetarian hotpot 58
Vegetarian pasties 52
Vegetables. *See also* Bean, etc.
  Mediterranean vegetables 60
  Spiced vegetables and rice 59

Zucchini:
  Baked zucchini 64
  Minted zucchini with peas and corn 61

Acknowledgments

Recipes devised by Rhona Newman
Photography by Rex Bamber
Food prepared by Caroline Ellwood